Fearless
creativity

Beth Mende Conny

Blue Island

Blue Island Productions • Frederick, MD

Fearless creativity

Unleash your creativity

Tap your talents

Crash through blocks

Silence naysayers

Gain mastery

Live your dreams

Beth Mende Conny

Blue Island Productions
Frederick, MD

Contents

Creativity is infinite

It is ever available. It seeks expression. It *needs* us. But not just our ideas. It needs us to rediscover the world; to clean life's dusty corners and buff its dull surfaces.

Creativity wants us to get comfortable with the uncomfortable, to toss out our assumptions and expectations, to find a way not just out but in. It wants us to be lighter and younger, whatever our age, to look around each day and say, "Well, I'll be darned!"

Creativity wants us to love and like and simply get along. To listen with our hearts. To appreciate the incredible complexity and simplicity of life — and how it all boils down to this:

To live is to create. To create is to live fearlessly.
                                    — *Beth Mende Conny*

Chapter 1
Be fearless

Being creative is our nature and right — our way of saying to the world, I am here. I matter.
        — Beth Mende Conny

I am creative and I am fearless. Not all of the time, alas, or in equal proportions. Some days I am sizzling hot, unstoppable and, quite honestly, brilliant. Fear can't get a shot off. Other days, fear rams its way into my life, hell bent on destroying my confidence and the projects to which I've given my heart and time.

Most days, however — and this is important to note — I manage to keep the two balanced. It's no small feat and there's still a lot of wobbling going on. Nonetheless I trudge on, even happily skip along. I have *learned* to do so. I have no choice. Life is too short and the list of my lifelong dreams is too long.

I suspect you feel the same way. That you, too, have a list of dreams you have yet to make true. So what's stopping you? Time? Money? Inexperience? There's always something, be it real or imagined, and you can't let that something stand in your way. True, you must live within certain constraints; I certainly do. But oftentimes constraints are fears in disguise. Remove the disguise and you unleash the forces that bring dreams to life.

Fearless Creativity will help you do just that. *Do* is the operative word here. This two-letter word packs a punch. It's more powerful than the following 10 words combined, words that too often represent the progression of our dreams: *wish, plan, dabble, procrastinate, attempt, abandon, chastise, justify, mourn, regret.* Fear feeds off of this progression, gaining strength from it while sapping yours. Please don't let this happen. The stakes are too high. Give in to fear and you hand over your best: *You* — the person you long for and were meant to be.

Here's where *Fearless Creativity* steps in. My role is to help you move beyond the fear that stands between you and your dreams. Write a novel, move overseas, earn an advanced degree, start a nonprofit, buy a farm, become a stand-up comic — these, among others, are the dreams that make your heart sing. But you have been humming their tunes for far too long. It is time to act, and I am here to gently prod and not-so-gently push you to do so.

I will be your guide, therapist and resident nag. I will help you identify your dearest of dreams, so you may harness your creative energies and develop realistic, fail-proof strategies to achieve them. I'll show you where to find the time, space and cheerleaders your efforts require. I'll take you beyond your mental blocks, so you may gain insight and momentum. And I will show you how to apply all you learn to other aspects of your life, so your life, itself, becomes a creative act.

The tips and tools I share *work*. I can vouch for each, not just because I created them but because I use them: some daily, others occasionally, others when I am stuck and need to bring out the big guns. They'll work for you too *if* you follow these rules:

Take yourself and your dreams seriously
Or at least go through the motions. Read a few chapters, do a few exercises and you'll feel a creative shift.

Go slowly
Zipping through *Fearless Creativity* won't fast-track your process. In fact, it may slow it down. You'll need time-outs to think, regroup and, literally, rest.

Begin at the beginning
All chapters in *Fearless Creativity* can stand alone. Nonetheless, I strongly suggest you read Chapters 1–4 in consecutive order. They are the foundation upon which the rest of the book is built.

Use the quotations
At the end of each chapter, you will find quotes to inspire and guide your efforts. You may find it helpful to adopt one as your daily, weekly or monthly theme.

Don't stop
In the Appendix, I've included blank copies of all of the charts and lists in *Fearless Creativity*. Use these should you need extra space or when you undertake a new venture.

Enough of the rules, let's dive in.

Be fearless!

Fortune favors the audacious.
> — *Erasmus*

Chase down your passion like it's the last bus of the night.
> — *Terri Guillemets*

Courage is doing what you're afraid to do. There can be no courage unless you are scared.
> — *Eddie Rickenbacker*

Take risks. Safeway is a grocery store.
> — *Joey Reiman*

Courage is the power to let go of the familiar.
> — *Mary Bryant*

Don't be afraid of your fears. They're not there to scare you. They're there to let you know that something is worth it.
> — *C. JoyBell C*

Life shrinks or expands in proportion to one's courage.
> — *Anais Nin*

Chapter 2
Tap your creativity

What if the very reason you were created was to be creative?
—Michelle Dennis Evans

The human brain has two sides, or hemispheres. The left hemisphere processes information in an analytical and linear manner, which makes it particularly good at tasks involving words, music, math and memorization. Detailed-oriented, it sees components first and then arranges them logically into a whole.

The brain's right hemisphere processes information in a visual and intuitive manner, which makes it particularly good at creative thinking and artistic projects. It first views things holistically (I prefer the term *whole-istically*) and then sees its parts.

Although the left and right brains differ, one is not superior to the other. Sure, one hemisphere may be dominant (or domineering), but that does not mean they can't work as a team. In fact, they must, for to be fearlessly creative, you need to tap *all* of your brainpower. So let's get tapping.

Creativity defined

Before we discuss proven strategies for becoming fearlessly creative, let's talk about creativity itself. Here's Wikipedia's definition:

... the phenomenon whereby a person creates something new (a product, a solution, a work of art, a novel, a joke, etc.) that has some kind of value. What counts as "new" may be in reference to the individual creator, or to the society or domain within which the novelty occurs. What counts as "valuable" is similarly defined in a variety of ways.

Hmm. Quite the left-brained definition, don't you think? Let's hop over to the right brain for a different perspective.

Right-brainer that I am, I believe creativity is a different sort of noun and certainly a more active, enlivened one. I think of creativity as a state of being — the essence of who we are. It is an acknowledgement of our many gifts and, more important, that we are alive.

Here's another great thing about creativity: It thinks we're wonderful, so wonderful, in fact, that it would love to spend more time with us. It doesn't care if we are at our desk, behind the wheel, lying in bed, standing at the sink or in line at the supermarket. It doesn't care if we have the flu or the blues, are on a deadline or in the shower. It doesn't care if it is 3 a.m. or p.m., Monday or Saturday. It just wants to hang out with us, most especially with you.

You, of course, are more than just you. Given the many hats you wear, you are several people crammed into one and each is battling for position. Creativity, however, is a gentle soul. It doesn't like elbowing its way into the tumult of your everyday life. Rather, it waits patiently for things to settle down and then ... tap, tap, tap on your shoulder, whisper in your ear: "Pssst. Want to get away for a bit? I've got this great idea!" Is that incredible or what? That depends on your response. *If* you even hear what creativity has to say.

De-habit your life
We are all pilots — autopilots. We fly, as we live, according to our habits. Some habits are good. They are the shorthand of our

everyday lives. Without them, we would waste lots of time and would most certainly get to work late. Can you imagine if you woke up and first had to figure out what to do and how to do it? Take shaving, for example. Unless you are a novice, you do not have to think about how to lather up or hold a razor. You've been at it for years and likely shave the same way every day, one cheek before the other. Ditto for putting on your deodorant and shoes, and engaging in most other daily routines.

To be creative, however, you need to break your routines. This is harder than you think. In fact, it's disorienting, not to mention uncomfortable. You are thrust into the Great (and not-so-great) Unknown. And what is waiting for you there? Fear.

Think I am being dramatic? This book is about fearless creativity, after all, not about changing your shaving habits. But de-habiting is central to fearlessness. You've got to get off of autopilot if you are to change how you think. The "De-habit List" that follows will begin the process. Warning: This seemingly easy exercise is hard!

De-habit exercise

Step 1
On the *De-habit List* which follows, list five morning tasks you do on autopilot. Some examples:

• Brush your upper teeth before your lowers

• Put your left shoe on before your right

• Button your shirt from top to bottom

• Put your right earring on before your left

• Slip your wristwatch onto your left wrist

Step 2

Now review your list and identify the tasks that *must* be performed the same way every day. I'm going to guess (hope) that none are that rigid. That means you can shake up your daily routine without dire consequences. So, let's have you do so.

Choose one habit to de-habit for three days. For example, brush your bottom teeth first, button your shirt from bottom to top, etc. (Looking for a real challenge? Try sleeping on the opposite side of the bed. Killer.)

Guaranteed — de-habiting will feel strange. Indeed, you may hate it, and don't be surprised if you slip back onto autopilot. Nonetheless, you will get a sense of the powerful hold even mundane habits can have on our lives. Imagine then how the power of our mental habits — namely those that determine how we navigate our lives — forms our limited perceptions and emboldens our fears.

De-habit List

1. _____

2. _____

3. _____

4. _____

5. _____

As Albert Einstein said, "You can't keep doing the same thing and expect a different result." And so it is with habitual thinking. You can't keep thinking the same thoughts and expect to build creative muscle; you've got to re-route your mind.

Re-route your mind

Neurons are the building blocks of our nervous system. We have 100 billion of them and their job is to transmit information. New information, new pathways. New pathways, increased ability to learn, adapt and remember. Scientists once believed this building process occurred only in infancy. They now know it occurs at all stages of life. The most important stage? From my perspective: *now*. Now is the time to grow our brains, to feed them a healthy diet of new ideas and experiences so we can build mental muscle, gain confidence and learn to fear less.

But too often we feed our minds empty calories: hackneyed loops from childhood; mind-numbing YouTube videos; unengaging social engagements; habitual actions that lock us into an ever-shrinking world. It doesn't take much to expand our minds and create new pathways, however. Here are suggestions:

Schedule time to daydream

Daydreams enable our minds to wander, discover new lands and make surprising connections. From them come the ah-ha's that inspire and shape our lives. When used purposefully, they create the state of mind in which creativity thrives.

Lately, I've been giving myself 10 minutes daily simply to sit on the couch and daydream; it has become its own form of meditation. I set my phone alarm, put up my feet and allow my thoughts to traipse down roads less traveled. (I keep a notepad and pen within reach, should an idea want to stop and chat.)

Mundane tasks can also get my creative juices flowing. For example, I hate washing dishes. Yet sometimes the repetitive nature of soaping, scrubbing and rinsing puts me in a dreamy state. That's why I've gotten so many great ideas at the kitchen sink. Many others have come while commuting, grocery shopping and shoveling snow. By reframing the value of such mundane tasks, I can get into their flow. When undertaking them, I'll often give myself a prompt like, "What's the best way to organize Chapters X and Y?" or "What's the one thing I can do today to work through my block?" From experience I know that a well-phrased question is like a heat-seeking missile. It finds its mark — an answer — even if the answer takes a few days or weeks to germinate.

Note: Avoid yes-no questions because they provide little useful information. Too, ask empowering questions: "How can I strengthen my writing?" vs. "Why am I such a crummy writer?"

Read arbitrarily
Consider me old-fashioned, but I still believe books grow the mind. They grant me access to worlds beyond the circle of my everyday life. I particularly like nonfiction books on topics I know nothing about. In fact, I make a game of it. Why don't you play along?

- Turn your birthdate into a Dewey Decimal Number and then locate a library book with that number. For example, if your birthday is Sept. 4, you could search under 094, 9.4, 9.40, etc.

- Go to the biography section and choose the very first or last book on the shelves. Or choose one with your last name (e.g., Smith) or the name of a family member.

- Go to the library's new books section and choose the first book you see that has a yellow binding or the number 10 in its title.

Learn from strangers
Most likely you interact with strangers over the course of your week, even if it is just to make eye contact. Now, I want you to engage

others in conversation so you can learn something interesting about them. For example, the person you speak with may have:

- Visited Somalia and escaped being kidnapped by pirates

- Lost his job, family and home because of his gambling

- Learned how to circumvent the IRS automated phone system

Set yourself a minimum quota of one conversation a week, which would equal 52 unique and interesting conversations a year. As a variation, conduct "how things work" interviews. Contact someone doing something interesting — animal rescue, screenwriting, rocket repair, etc. Ask meaty questions so you can view the world through a new lens.

Creativity, the guest

As I mentioned, creativity seeks our company. It behooves us, therefore, to extend it an invitation, not just once in a while but regularly, perhaps even daily. We do not have to sit and chit-chat at length or even chat at all. We simply have to be welcoming. Some suggestions:

Take note of the times you are most creative

My creative thoughts usually come in the early morning, while I am lying in bed and my mind is shifting from a sleeping to waking state. Thoughts trickle and then flood through my system. I race to my laptop and frantically type away, knowing that I have a narrow window of opportunity; by noon, I am out of ideas.

So what time of day does creativity visit you? Before breakfast? Early afternoon? Late at night when everyone else is asleep? Where will the visit most likely occur? At your desk or in your car? At the gym or in your shower? And what will you most likely be doing at the time? Jogging? Washing dishes? Reading on the couch? Identify patterns and you increase the likelihood of creativity dropping by.

Accept the gifts creativity leaves behind

Even if you are unwelcoming, creativity leaves gifts for you to enjoy and use: fragments of ideas, snippets of sentences, pearls of wisdom strung into long necklaces. It is a shame (practically a crime!) to not accept these gifts or, at least, store them in a safe place. For example, you can:

- Jot your ideas onto whatever paper is within reach — notepads, napkins, backs of receipts, etc. — and then stick them in a dedicated "ideas" file folder or box.

- Journal at length or compress your ideas into key phrases that can be decompressed later.

- Create a portable office by filling a large plastic bag with pens, highlighters, binder clips, stickies, notebooks and other items. Carry it with you, so you're ready to capture ideas whenever and wherever an idea appears.

- Stock bedside supplies so you're ready to roll when ideas wake you in the middle of the night. These include a flashlight and extra batteries; extra pillows, so you can prop up in bed; a pen that writes upside down, should you prefer to lay down while brainstorming; headphones to listen to mood music, etc.

- Dictate ideas into a digital recorder or use a voice recognition app on your phone, tablet or computer. Leave yourself a voicemail.

- Create a mind map to capture idea spin-offs and interrelationships.

- Sit quietly and simply *absorb* the ideas. You will be surprised by how many will stay with you long after you have moved on to (or been sucked into) other activities.

Whatever your method, don't worry about ordering your ideas; that comes later. Nor should you judge their value or feasibility.

That comes later, as well. For now, just open yourself to the gifts creativity brings.

Trust your creativity

Creativity is always present, whether you notice it or not. It is the ah-ha! moment in the middle of the night; the gnawing sense that you should or could do something differently (and that you will). It is taking a new route home simply because you feel like it or grabbing a camera to photograph a sunset. It is sitting down to journal and winding up with a poem; dying your hair blue on one side, red on the other, then changing it back. It is allowing yourself to do nothing but listen to that voice that says, "Hey, want to hear a great idea?"

So acknowledge your creativity; draw it close. Let it be your ally as you pursue your dreams and face your fears.

Tap your creativity!

Creativity is intelligence having fun.
— *Albert Einstein*

The creative act, the defeat of habit by originality, overcomes everything.
— *George Lois*

When we create, we become more than the sum of our parts.
— *Yanni*

Make an empty space in any corner of your mind, and creativity will fill it.
— *Dee Hock*

If we all did the things we are capable of, we would astound ourselves.
— *Thomas Edison*

A hunch is creativity trying to tell you something.
— *Frank Capra*

Chapter 3
Challenge your fears

Fear is blasphemy. It disrespects the sacred, namely, you.
—Beth Mende Conny

Fear is important and necessary. It keeps us from darting across a street during rush hour traffic or jumping out of a plane without a parachute. It makes us run from charging tigers and tsunamis. But fear has a dark side. It holds us prisoner, freezes us in time. It shouts and whispers, nags and whimpers. It is Muzak, surround-sound, a pain in the ass. Fear sees the world in black and white, searches for the bad in all people, places, things and ideas. It hoards compliments and bursts balloons. Worse: Fear is blasphemy. It disrespects the sacred, namely, you.

What scares you?
When it comes to fear, one size does not fit all. Nor is fear singular. We each have several, perhaps many, fears, and they are as specific to us as our genes. Identifying them is important because otherwise we don't know which we are dealing with, when or why. Recognize our fears and their triggers, and we can better understand and engage them.

And that's why we will begin this chapter with the exercise *I am afraid that/of ...* Its goal is simple: to become familiar with your fears and how, if unaddressed, they will prevent you from bringing your dreams to life.

Instructions

- List your most potent fears, one fear to each line. Do not self-edit or judge yourself. A fear is a fear is a fear. No one is looking over your shoulder and challenging you. No one will even see this list, unless you so choose. Do a mind dump. Get into the dusty corners of your mind where fears often hide.

- Next, review your list and ask yourself the following questions for each fear.

Is the fear fact-based?

Namely, is its outcome inevitable? Say, for example, you want to be an actress but fear going to auditions; you fear you will be turned down for a part. (Note that I used the words *turned down*, not *rejected*. That's because directors are not *rejecting* anyone. Rather, they are looking for a *specific* personality type for a *specific* role. It isn't personal.)

But being turned down isn't inevitable. It isn't *fact*, the way the earth's rotation is fact. Too often we live by such facts and, knowingly or not, back off of our dreams.

Is the fear situational?

In other words, is your fear a constant companion or is it triggered at certain times, in certain places or by certain people? For instance, if you are afraid of heights, you likely won't have a problem walking down a street (unless, perhaps, you are in San Francisco). If you are on the 97th floor of a skyscraper, however, your heart may start to beat wildly. If you are thinking about changing careers and share the news with negative thinkers, a chorus of fears may start singing in your ears.

I am afraid that/of ...

Is the fear optional?

Some fears are thrust upon us. If you live in a war-torn city, for example, you likely fear violence. And for good reason. No matter what precautions you take to protect yourself — buy a gun, stay indoors — your circumstances are beyond your control.

But not all fears are compulsory. To a great extent, we pick and choose them. If you want to scuba dive off the coast of Oahu, Hawaii, you will have to deal with your fear of sharks. If you want to run for political office, you have to deal with the possibility of losing an election.

Is the fear yours?

Sometimes people will impose their fears on you, shooting worst-case scenarios at you like poison darts. These fear-mongers may be threatened by or jealous of you, and there is little you can do but avoid them. My sense is that most people are not ill-willed; rather, they are merely afraid. They project their fears onto us because they, themselves, are afraid.

Parents are great examples of this. (FYI: I'm a parent.) Because they love us, they try to protect us from the big, bad world. Sometimes, however, they only feel safe when they make us afraid enough to stay within their protective reach. Their fear is *theirs*, not ours, even though they try to hand it off.

Is the fear shared?

As noted, our fears are unique and, thereby, are woven into the fabric of our lives. Nonetheless, we are all cut from the same cloth. We all eat, sleep, breathe ... and fear. Shared fears are born of common experience, influenced by economics, political upheavals, technological changes and natural disasters, among many, many other things. In this sense, they are realistic and often to be expected. What you may think as unique is not.

Is the fear specific?

Say, for example, you have decided to return to school to complete your A.A. degree. You are afraid you will not do well. But what does not doing well mean? That you will not have time to study? That you will do poorly because you do not know how to conduct research or write a term paper? That everyone will be smarter than you? All of the above?

In this case, your fear is actually several fears in one. Your first task, therefore, is to distinguish among them so you can tackle them individually.

Is the fear important?

Some fears are more potent than others, but that doesn't make them more important. I may be terrified of sharks, but if I have no real interest in scuba diving, I can cast it off (or at least try to). If I fear intimacy but want to be in a loving relationship, I am going to have to face that fear head-on. The stakes are higher. Accordingly, differentiating among and between your fears allows you to limit their number and conserve energy.

What are you NOT afraid of?

Opposites help us better understand the world. Without day, we would not know night. Ditto for up/down, in/out, left/right. Each defines the other.

Not so fear and courage. They coexist. They are, in fact, a dynamic duo. Without their push and pull, we would remain stationary, become stagnant. Our dreams would die.

Courage moves *with* fear toward a goal. Therefore, it is important for you to acknowledge not just your fears but your courageous acts. Some acts are awe-inspiring: you've sailed solo around the world or founded one of the world's largest corporations. Others are personal: you've survived breast cancer or entered a talent contest. Still others are so woven into your everyday life that you overlook them. You have forgotten all the courage it took to master them, such as to learn how to walk, drive a car or raise your hand in class.

All of which is to say, you are more courageous than you think — and you've got a track record to prove it. On the *Acts of Courage* worksheet, you'll put these feats in writing.

Instructions

- List actions that required courage on your part. Don't compare yourself to others, however. Courage is relative.

- Choose different types of acts:
  - Public acts, namely, those you did in front of others (e.g., performed at an open mic night)
  - Private acts (e.g., took a lower-paying but more socially meaningful job)
  - Everyday acts (e.g., began a daily exercise routine)

- As you bring your dreams to life add them to your *Acts of Courage* list. It will help counter the inevitable fears that arise when you move into new territory.

- Review your list every week or so to remind yourself you're braver than you think. In the process, you will become your own role model.

Acts of Courage

_____

_____

_____

_____

_____

_____

_____

_____

_____

_____

_____

Challenge your fears!

Failure is an event, never a person.
                                    —*William D. Brown*

It's not how far you fall, but how high you bounce that counts.
                         — *Zig Ziglar*

The only real mistake is the one from which we learn nothing.
                         — *Henry Ford*

Failure is the condiment that gives success its flavor.
                         — *Truman Capote*

Doubt kills more dreams than failure ever will.
                         — *Suzy Kassem*

The sun won't shine unless you put away the umbrella.
                         — *Unknown*

Daring is not saying, "I'm willing to risk failure." Daring is saying, "I know I will eventually fail and I'm still in."
                         —*Brené Brown*

Try again. Fail again. Fail better.
                         —*Samuel Beckett*

Chapter 4
Awaken your dreams

Trust your future to the things you love.
— Diane Sawyer

To bring a dream to fruition, you must wake it up, pull it out of bed and dress it in work clothes. Only then can you give the dream the shape, substance and specificity it needs to succeed.

It helps to think of dreams as projects; each has a unique beginning and end. No two projects are created equal, however. Some are simply better than others. The better ones touch our hearts, open our minds, help us gain mastery and confidence, and move us closer to our dreams. The lesser ones are uninspiring and overly demanding. They have us moving in circles, bumping into walls and stumbling over our insecurities. We don't like where they are headed; heck, we don't even like their company. It should come as no surprise then that we have to be careful about choosing the projects that are most worthy of our time and energy.

That effort, like a marriage, requires commitment, so marry well. But don't worry about making the perfect choice. Like you, your dream project will have its shortcomings and quirks. But as long as its pros outweigh its cons, you've upped the odds of its completion.

But how do you choose Mr. or Ms. Right among your dream projects? The exercises in this chapter will make the choice evident.

Dream Projects

On the *Dream Projects* worksheet, list any and all of your dream projects. They do not need to be fully detailed or developed, or even current; some projects may be worth dusting off. Do not prioritize them, which we will do later. And don't exclude projects that are beyond your present abilities and circumstances. Who you are now is not who you will be months, weeks or even days from now.

Note: Although you don't have to complete your list in one sitting, give yourself a cut-off point or you will be adding projects ad infinitum. You will find additional copies of the *Dream Projects* worksheet in the Appendix.

Below is a sample list, which I'll pretend is mine. In fact, some of the listings are mine.

- Write novel
- Run for city council
- Play in the WNBA
- Open bakery
- Ski down Mt. Everest
- Move to Ireland
- Design and build own home
- Get Ph.D. in American history
- Learn Italian
- Run marathon
- Win Powerball
- Change careers
- Join Peace Corps
- Ride bike across Canada

Dream Projects

- Launch writing program for people with disabilities
- Create educational apps for children
- Be happy

Making the cut, Round #1

The list above has 17 dream projects on it. Great as they may be, there is no way I could work on each simultaneously, let alone over the course of my lifetime. Obviously, I will have to delete some projects from my list, but how?

First, I will delete projects that are not serious contenders. I do not really want to be a politician. (Who wants to be reviled?) Nor do I really want to bike ride across Canada (too hard), move to Ireland (would miss my family) or open a bakery (too many hours). As for joining the Peace Corps, the idea doesn't have the same appeal it did when I graduated college. I am now married with children.

Second, I will nix projects I would not undertake unless someone paid me a million bucks or I was drunk (e.g., ski down Mt. Everest). Third, I will delete projects that I, myself, wouldn't want to pursue but would love to have others do so for me — and pay me a commission. And so I will delete my idea for developing a series of educational children's apps. Fourth, I will delete projects that fall into the hobby category. For example, learning Italian would be fun, but I have no real interest in devoting hours to it.

Fifth, I will nix unrealistic ideas. For example, although I have fantasized about playing in the WNBA, I'm a 5'3" woman who cannot dribble and is well past her basketball prime. Winning Powerball also is unrealistic because doing so relies on chance, not effort (except to buy tickets). True, the more I play, the greater my chances; nonetheless, the likelihood of winning is millions to one.

Sixth, and finally, I will nix ideas that are not ideas as much as ideals. "To be happy," for example, is a state of being, not a project with a quantifiable goal, such as getting a Ph.D. in American History. Nor can it be achieved once and for all; happiness comes and goes.

Using the above as guidance, the number of my dream project ideas has shrunk from 17 to six:

• Write novel

• Design and build own home

• Get Ph.D. in American history

• Run a marathon

• Change careers

• Launch a writing program for people with disabilities

Now it's your turn to evaluate the projects you listed on your *Dream Projects* worksheet. Cross off those that aren't serious contenders. Transfer the remainders onto the *Dream Project Criteria Worksheet*, which follows my sample worksheet. You'll find additional worksheets in the Appendix.

Making the cut, Round #2
Now the fun part: You're going to identify your Mr. or Ms. Right among your dream projects, using the *Dream Project Criteria Worksheet*. The worksheet will help you determine objectively your interest in a project and your ability to bring it to fruition. The exercise has no rights or wrongs. It simply reflects your interests and circumstances *at this point in your life.*

Instructions
• Assign a numeric score of 1-10 for each idea listed on your *Dream Project Criteria Worksheet*; 1 will be the lowest score possible, and 10 will be the highest. Your scores will be based on these five criteria: Expertise, Money, Time, Support and Passion. I describe each criterion on pages 30-33.

Beth's **Dream Project Criteria Worksheet**

Projects	Expertise	Money	Time	Support	Passion	TOTALS
Write novel						
Design & build own home						
Get Ph.D. in American History						
Run marathon						
Change careers						
Launch writing program for people with disabilities						
TOTALS						

Your Dream Project Criteria Worksheet

Projects	Expertise	Money	Time	Support	Passion	TOTALS
TOTALS						

- When scoring your ideas, I strongly suggest you do so one criterion at a time. In other words, rate all of your ideas by the criterion "Expertise," then by "Money," then by "Time," etc. It will hasten the process so you don't overthink your responses. Generally, scores that come to mind first are the most accurate.

- You can work through the exercise as often as you'd like, adding to or deleting from your list of dream projects. Again, you will find extra blank worksheets in the Appendix.

Criteria descriptions

#1 — Expertise

All projects require expertise, be it specific skills, experience or know-how. For example, if you want to open a bakery, you need to know something about baking. You may already have that expertise; namely, you now work in a bakery. But that doesn't mean you know how to run a business. This is not to say that you have to know everything *now*; you will never know everything anyway. At the minimum, however, you need a willingness to learn.

Accordingly, on a scale from 1-10, rate your level of expertise and/or your willingness to develop it. For example, if I know enough to launch a bakery, I might give myself an 8. If I know nothing, I might give myself a 1. *However*, if despite my lack of knowledge I am committed to learning everything required, I might rate myself a 9. Again, your score should be based not just on expertise but a willingness to gain it.

#2 — Money

All projects require some sort of financial expenditure. If you want to build a vacation home, you'll need to purchase a piece of property, raise funds for permits and taxes, wood, nails, steel-toed work boots, etc. You may already have these things or have extended family members who are willing to pitch in, in which case you might give yourself a 10.

Or you may have zero bucks. In that instance, you must ask yourself: "How willing am I to raise the funds I need? Am I willing to get a second job, purchase a smaller plot of land or build in a less desirable area? Am I willing to learn carpentry so I can do a lot of the work myself?"

On a scale from 1-10, rate your ability to financially support your projects *or* your willingness to raise the requisite capital. (In an example like the one above, elbow grease *is* capital.)

#3 — Time

No matter how much time you have — days, months, years — you will always need more. After all, there are only 24 hours in a day. Excluding the approximate eight hours you sleep, you've got only 16 hours to work with. That's not a lot given all you must cram into that time: eat, shower, work, commute, cook, clean, help kids with homework, go to the dentist, return holiday gifts, mow the lawn, walk the dog, fight unauthorized credit card charges, visit an ailing relative … breathe.

If you are lucky, you have these pockets (or slivers) of time to devote to your dream project. If you are working toward a Ph.D., for example, you may be able to study on the bus to work, take Internet courses or turn your two-week vacation into a two-week stint in the library. Or you may drop out of school to work two jobs and save enough money to finish your education uninterrupted at a later date.

Accordingly, on a scale from 1-10, rate how much time you have or are willing to find to complete your project.

#4 — Personal support

Rare is the dream project that doesn't affect others in some way. Chucking the corporate world to write a novel, for example, may not have the same appeal to your spouse as it does to you, especially if he or she is expected to become the breadwinner or to take over cooking, cleaning and child care duties.

But that doesn't mean you can't get support elsewhere. You may in fact have a squad of cheerleaders: friends, colleagues, instructors or mentors. Or you may find the support you need from individuals you don't know personally. Public figures, experts, writers, artists, inventors or celebrities — their past or present words, actions and life stories may be sufficient inspiration as you build your confidence and skills. Another source of support? *You*. For whatever your project, you will spend some time, perhaps a considerable amount, working by yourself and thinking for yourself.

On a scale from 1-10, rate your level of personal support. Do you have, or could you create, a dedicated crew of cheerleaders? How willing are you to fly solo, to lend yourself the support you may not get from others?

#5 — Passion

Passion is the fuel that drives a dream project. Without it, a project sputters along, traveling a road that lacks scenery. Sure you can tell yourself a particular road is worth taking because it's toll-free and a straight shot, but you probably can't convince yourself it is the best route.

Say, for example, you want to change jobs. You put in for a promotion or a transfer, or maybe you decide to jump ship. Maybe you become a consultant and rake in the bucks. But what if what you want is not to change your job but your career? What if becoming a teacher is the route you really want to take?

Unfortunately, passion alone can't get you where you want to go. Expertise, time, money and personal support — all are essential; each can be quantified. Not so passion. It is nebulous. But that doesn't make it unimportant. In fact, it may be the most important of all considerations.

Accordingly, on a scale from 1-10, rate how passionate you are about each of your projects.

Final step
Using my completed *Dream Project Criteria Worksheet* as a model, total your scores for each of your dream projects, as well as for each criterion. Once done, we can interpret your scores.

Interpreting your dream project scores

As noted, the *Dream Project Criteria Worksheet* objectively gauges your interest in a project idea and your ability to bring it to fruition. High and low scores are equally important; together, they offer insight into your projects — and you.

Individual project scores

Review the total scores for each of your projects. Did any receive a perfect 50? An imperfect 5? Although there are no right or wrong scores, total ratings of 25 or less should set off alarms. Something about these projects is "off," and it's important to determine what that something is.

I admit I was surprised by some of my scores. For example, I hadn't realized how little passion I had for getting a Ph.D. (15 out of 50) or designing and building my own home (7), even though both had been on my list for years. As for changing careers, it was so nonspecific I couldn't rate it at all. Too, as I pondered my scores, I realized that what I really wanted was to apply my skills in new ways. That would explain my two highest overall scores: to write a novel (40) and to launch writing programs for individuals with disabilities (44).

Criteria scores

Criteria score totals are important because they reflect how ready, willing or able you are to undertake not just *one* project but *any* project.

For example, if your "Support" scores are low, you may have to rethink your relationships. Negative people generally are not upbeat about their own lives, let alone yours. If being around them deflates you, one of your first orders of business is to expand your network, something I cover at length in Chapter 7, "Recruit cheerleaders." If your "Time" scores are consistently low, you may need to reevaluate not just your schedule but priorities; something has to change somewhere. I offer suggestions in Chapter 6, "Protect your time."

If your "Money" scores are low, you may have to tighten your belt or get financial assistance. If your "Expertise" scores are low, you may need to do some soul searching: Are you choosing projects that are beyond reach or are you judging yourself too harshly?

Of all the criteria, "Passion" is the most important. With passion, you can, indeed will, find a way to get the expertise, time, money and support you need. Passion is the engine that drives action.

And the winner is ...

Now that you have rated all of your ideas, choose your winner. This is the idea you will bring to fruition. Step by step, the remaining chapters will show you how.

Beth's **Dream Project Criteria Worksheet**

Projects	Expertise	Money	Time	Support	Passion	TOTALS
Write novel	7	9	6	10	8	40
Design & build own home	1	1	1	1	3	7
Get Ph.D. in American History	5	6	1	2	1	15
Run marathon	4	10	5	10	1	30
Change careers	?	?	?	?	?	0
Launch writing program for people with disabilities	9	9	6	10	10	44
TOTALS	26	35	19	33	23	

Awaken your dreams!

Passion is the genesis of genius.
> — *Anthony Robbins*

The most powerful weapon on earth is the human soul on fire.
> — *Ferdinand Foch*

One person with passion is better than forty people merely interested.
> — *E.M. Forster*

Harness your power to your passion. Honor your calling.
> — *Oprah Winfrey*

Someday is not a day of the week.
> — *Unknown*

At first dreams seem impossible, then improbable, then inevitable.
> — *Christopher Reeve*

Decisions are the hinges of destiny.
> — *Unknown*

Chapter 5
Strategize success

An idea not coupled with action will never get any bigger than the brain cell it occupied.

— *Scott Adams*

All projects have a beginning and end. The progression from one point to the other goes like this:

A — Z

When we think about the process a bit more, however, we realize that things are not that simple. The space between them is wider than we thought. It may look something like this:

A ———————————————— Z

It is at this point that many of us begin to get uncomfortable; the distance between A and Z seems too vast. We cannot imagine how we can get from one to the other, and so we turn our backs on our dreams. And feel awful. Another failure. Another example of our lack of courage.

If we hang in there, however, we begin to see that there are steps between the beginning and end:

A B C D E F G H I J K L M N O P Q R S T U V W X Y Z

Whew! An improvement — until we realize that the steps we must take are not linear. Rather, like kids in a playground, they are all over the place.

A B C D E F G H I J K L M N O P Q R S T U V W X Y Z

How, then, do we proceed? We give order to the messiness that is the creative process. We put the steps of our projects into sequential, left-brain order.

Identifying project steps

Any project comprises a series of steps, some big, some small, some enjoyable, some boring, etc. The greater your ability to divvy your project into steps, the greater the likelihood you will complete it.

To better understand this concept, let's use novel writing as an example. Say, I want to finish my novel (which I do). To achieve my goal, I must first write my book. (Details, details.) But what are the steps between "write book" and "finish book"? To identify them, I will list them on the *Beth's Project Steps* sheet.

I now have 13 steps, although I know their number will increase exponentially over the course of my project. I'm going to ignore that for now, however, because I don't want to get overwhelmed. Instead, I will evaluate each task to determine its priority order: beginning, middle or end, and then put a check mark in the appropriate box. Should steps be ongoing — i.e., "write book "— I will check additional columns.

Now it's your turn to complete your project steps list. Do a mind dump. (You'll find extra sheets in the Appendix.) Should you find yourself blocking, I've listed some prompts on page 40.

Beth's **Project Steps**

Steps

Steps	Beginning	Middle	End
Write book	✓	✓	
Get agent			✓
Research locations	✓		
Outline book	✓		
Write up book proposal			✓
Edit book		✓	
Find critiquers		✓	
Develop characters	✓		
Create filing system	✓		
Set up office space	✓		
Develop project budget	✓		
Read other novels	✓	✓	✓
Join writer's group	✓		

What do you need to do to ...
- schedule time off
- make travel plans
- get in physical shape
- identify contractors
- enter a degree program
- locate housing
- create a body of work
- develop expertise
- sharpen your skills
- find funding
- network with key players
- complete paperwork
- create prototype

Playing with a full deck

Review your steps and note how each has a distinct place in your project's progression. And so it is for my project, writing a novel, which can be summed up as follows:

Beginning steps
- Write book
- Research locations
- Outline book
- Develop characters
- Create filing system
- Set up office space
- Develop project budget
- Read other novels
- Join writer's group

Middle steps
- Write book
- Edit book

Your **Project Steps**

Steps

	Beginning	Middle	End

- Find critiquers
- Read other novels

End steps
- Get agent
- Write up book proposal
- Read other novels

Understanding this priority order is critical if I am to stay *under*whelmed, for it allows me, as it will you, to put first things first and set aside the rest. Sometimes I use index cards to make this distinction more evident.

As my clients will tell you, I am a big fan of index cards because they help me prioritize. I assign one step to each card and then place each card into its respective pile: beginning, middle or end. I then rubber band the middle and end piles together and remove them from sight, to avoid distraction. With blinders on, I get down to the business at hand.

Create steps within steps

A project does not stall. *We* stall. Often it's because the steps we have identified are simply too big. To regain momentum, we will need to create steps within steps.

For example, one of my beginning steps in writing my novel is to organize my project files. But there's more to the process than I once thought. For example, I will need a filing cabinet, file folders and labels. I also will need to rearrange my office to accommodate the cabinet. Too, I will need to develop a basic filing system. Without one, I won't know where to file or how to retrieve information. No wonder I kept putting off organizing my project. It was *not* a single step but several masquerading as one.

Every step has steps within steps, which themselves can be ordered into beginning, middle and end tasks. The greater your ability to differentiate among and between tasks, the greater your momentum. Even the smallest of steps moves you closer to your dreams.

Strategize success!

If you don't know exactly where you're going, how will you know when you get there?

> — *Steve Maraboli*

Goals are dreams with deadlines.

> — *Diana Scharf Hunt*

A goal properly set is halfway reached.

> — *Zig Ziglar*

In real life, strategy is actually very straightforward. You pick a general direction and implement like hell.

> — *Jack Welch*

Small steps, giant leaps — each moves you forward.

> — *Beth Mende Conny*

If you don't know where you are going, you'll end up someplace else.

> — *Yogi Berra*

Intention + attention = miracles

> — *Unknown*

Chapter 6
Protect your time

Why do we have trouble finding time but no problem wasting it?
— Beth Mende Conny

Managing time is like managing people — a tricky business. Hours, minutes, seconds have minds of their own. They don't care what you want. They don't care if you cajole and bribe them, yell and threaten or imprison them in cubicles. They will escape the moment you drop your guard. It is their nature to run.

Do not try to catch them. Days, hours, minutes — they are faster than you. As for seconds — forget it. They dash so quickly they become mere specks and then disappear. And we ask ourselves, as we do at the end of so many days, "Where has time gone?"

But we already know the answer. It has slipped into the dailyness of everyday life. Nonetheless, we sense that the elusive creature we call Time is, in fact, near; that if we dare step off the beaten path we have paved, we will hear it whisper, "I am here." And we must then decide to stay our course or change the trajectory of our lives.

Where does time go?

As a writer, I am often surprised by the assumptions people make about how I work. They imagine me holed up in my room for long stretches of time, telephone off and a do-not-disturb sign on the door. Uninterrupted, my creative juices flow until the hour when the midnight oil runs out and I stumble to bed, only to wake at dawn and begin yet again. Page after page, chapter after chapter, book after book, I write for hours while the world quietly waits at a respectful distance.

While this has some appeal (to me as well), it's true only in small part. I am not nearly as disciplined or creative as that, the world frequently interrupts me and I am asleep by 10:30 p.m. Further, I rarely get huge swaths of time in which to work. But I'm not complaining. I'd rather have crumbs — the pieces of time life metes out — than have no time at all. I'll take whatever is available. If I waited for just the right time, in just the right amount, I would never get anything done. Use it or lose it.

All of which is to say that you do not need huge blocks of time to get your project going, at least not initially. Even slivers will do because your efforts add up, much like pennies in a piggybank.

To find these slivers, you have to find where they disappeared. You can do so by using the *Daily Activities Log*. (You'll find additional logs in the Appendix.)

Instructions

Choose what you think is a typical day in your life and jot down what you do, and when. Approximations are fine. Examples:

- Time you wake up and go to sleep
- Morning routines (shower, get on treadmill, pray, read paper)
- Eat breakfast, lunch and dinner

Daily Activities Log

12 a.m.	12 p.m.
1 a.m.	1 p.m.
2 a.m.	2 p.m.
3 a.m.	3 p.m.
4 a.m.	4 p.m.
5 a.m.	5 p.m.
6 a.m.	6 p.m.
7 a.m.	7 p.m.
8 a.m.	8 p.m.
9 a.m.	9 p.m.
10 a.m.	10 p.m.
11 a.m.	11 p.m.

- Work
- Commute
- Run errands
- Help children with homework
- Answer email, post to Facebook
- Watch TV
- Read
- Listen to music
- Bedtime routines (brush teeth, choose next day's clothes)

Next up, complete the *Weekly Activities Log*.

Choose a typical week and create a summary of what you did each day. (Use your own sheets of paper to create a more detailed list; the greater the detail, the better.) Examples:

- Clean house
- Take continuing ed class
- Go shopping
- Visit in-laws
- Go to health club
- Ride bike
- Attend child's soccer game
- Do laundry
- Pay bills
- Get together with friends
- Community meetings

Now it is time to interpret your lists via armchair quarterbacking.

Weekly Activities Log

Sunday
Monday
Tuesday
Wednesday
Thursday
Friday
Saturday

Armchair quarterbacking

Armchair quarterbacks are people who tell others what they should do or should have done. We are all guilty of playing the part, whether or not we are sports fans. Although we may think of armchair quarterbacking as a negative thing, it can be a valuable time management tool if we use it on ourselves. It allows us to stand on the sidelines of our lives and make some judgment calls about how we are using our time — and how we are wasting it. And waste we do (including the time we complain about not having time). Enough already!

Accordingly, let's do some armchair quarterbacking. The goal is to help you identify where and how you may be wasting your time. First, review your daily and weekly log sheets and note where you put your energies. Second, ask yourself these questions for each of the listed activities:

- Is the activity mandatory, obligatory or optional? Who makes this determination? You? Your employer? Partner?

- Does it directly affect people? How important are these people to you?

- What is the worst that could happen if you stopped doing this activity?

- Does the activity support your long-term goals? The goals of loved ones, friends, coworkers, etc.?

- Does it add to, or detract from, your quality of life?

- Is it enjoyable? What would make it more so?

- Can it be delegated, if need be, even if it means it will not be according to your standards or that you will have to pay someone to do it?

- Are you doing the activity efficiently? If not, what improvements can be made?

- Do you have to do this activity *now*? If so, why?

- Does it always have to be done in the same way?

- What changes can you make to your schedule and/or life to reduce — or *increase* — its frequency?

The simple act of reviewing your daily and weekly activities will help you gain greater control of your day. Instead of being the armchair quarterback, you *become* the quarterback. You make the plays.

Finding time

The day my aunt graduated from college, with honors no less, was one of the high-points of her life. It had taken her 20 years — *20 years!* I cannot fathom how she kept at it, how anyone could. What's more amazing still is that she did it while raising two children and working part-time and full-time on occasions when my uncle was out of work. They had one car, which meant she could take only evening classes. It also meant she had to do all errands on foot, kids in tow; the supermarket was about a mile away. On weekends, she cooked and froze enough meals for the week. She went to bed shortly after her children did. She then set her alarm for midnight and studied until about 4 a.m. She caught a couple more hours of sleep and was then back at it. Twenty years!

I tell you her story because she is one of my inspirations. But her story also illustrates how, when necessary, we can find time to pursue a dream, even if it isn't under optimal conditions. And that raises an important question: Why do we have trouble finding time but no problem wasting it?

Time is always available to us. It's just a matter of looking for it. True, it may not come when we prefer or in the amount we need, nor may it be steady. But it is there nonetheless. So start looking for it. It certainly won't be looking for you.

At the very least, you can find occasional moments in the course of your day or week to at least *think* about your project. Below are suggestions for finding slivers of time in your personal life. Think of slivers you can find in your work life as well.

- Bring something project-related to keep you busy while waiting around (e.g., in your doctor's office or in line at the supermarket).

- While commuting, listen to podcasts, dictate ideas to yourself, mentally rehearse a particular task (e.g., putting up drywall, negotiating with your spouse about needing time to work on your project).

- Get up or go to bed a half-hour earlier or later.

- Swap childcare duties with your spouse, neighbors, etc. Form carpools to school, soccer practices, parties, etc.

- Combine interruptions (e.g., coordinate errands, check email once a day and at a set hour).

- Cut down on phone interruptions (e.g., do not answer the phone before or after a set time; get caller ID to avoid telemarketers).

- Get rid of anything you have to iron, sew, dry clean or wash in a special way and separately from other items. Do laundry every other week, even if it means buying extra underwear and socks.

- Buy and cook in bulk so you do not have to shop or prepare meals daily. Have your neighbor do the same and swap meals so neither of you has to cook one or two days a week.

- Have your children do the dishes, vacuuming and other household chores (no chores, no allowance or use of the family car).

- Cut back on newspapers and magazines. Skim headlines and table of contents to determine what is interesting/most important. Ignore the rest.

- Watch one less TV show. Record all shows to avoid commercials. Don't video stream movies that are longer than 90 minutes.

- Lower your standards. Question yourself every time the word *should* enters your mind ("I really should do/be... ").

Blackout days

So far we have talked about how we waste and find time. Now let's talk about how we distort it and the consequences this has on our projects.

Most simply, we distort time by elongating it, meaning, we stretch the distance between the beginning and end of our projects. We see the distance as being this:

A ———————————————————— Z

when it actually is shorter:

A ——————— Z

And we expect the impossible: that projects will flow at a steady, even pace. But projects rarely go according to plan. There are fits and starts. Steps that were to take a week or two, might take us three or four months, or even a year. Indeed, their progression may look like this:

A——— BCDEFGH—I—JK-L-MNOP—QRSTU—VW-X—YZ

Sometimes the fault is ours. Our plans are too ambitious or too optimistic. We do not factor in our learning curve or the curve balls life throws us: a stolen laptop, layoff, flooded basement, serious illness or death of a loved one. Nor do we factor in, let alone add to our calendars, predictable — indeed, cyclical — events. Even if you don't observe them, they affect your schedule. (Need convincing? Just ask a parent whose child is off of school between Christmas and New Year's.)

To prevent these *blackout* days from sneaking up on you, X them off your calendar, for you will accomplish little or no project work on them. Here are partial lists to get you started. Check all that apply.

Holidays
❏ New Year's Day
❏ Martin Luther King Day
❏ Valentine's Day
❏ Presidents Day
❏ Passover
❏ Easter
❏ Tax day
❏ Mother's Day
❏ Memorial Day
❏ Ramadan
❏ Father's Day
❏ Labor Day
❏ Rosh Hashana
❏ Yom Kippur

❏ Columbus Day
❏ Election Day
❏ Thanksgiving
❏ Chanukah
❏ Kwanza
❏ Christmas

Some events can be blacked out weeks or months ahead of time. Consider these:

❏ Birthdays
❏ Anniversaries
❏ Weddings
❏ Bar mitzvahs
❏ Vacations
❏ Family visits
❏ School events (parent-teacher conferences, scheduled closings, summer vacation)
❏ Sporting events (games, tournaments)
❏ Court dates
❏ Job transfers
❏ Corporate retreats/training/conferences
❏ Board meetings
❏ Church/synagogue/mosque events
❏ Fund-raising drives
❏ Dental cleanings
❏ Colonoscopies

Unfortunately some events cannot be blacked out because they are unpredictable, making them the ultimate monkey wrenches. For example: power outages, computer crashes, lost wallets/phones/ keys or, perhaps most frustrating of all, sick days (migraines, menstrual cramps, colds, allergies, sprained wrists, etc.). And let's not forget those low-energy days during which you procrastinate, block and feel sorry for yourself; days that require you to stay put so you can ponder, regroup or simply goof off.

So how do you deal with such events? You accept and prepare for them as much as possible. They are part of the creative process, business as usual. But while they contribute to your project's fits and starts, they need not make you lose focus. You can *always* control your attitude, even if you can't control your calendar. You can always better manage your time.

Protect your time!

I wish I could stand on a busy corner, hat in hand, and beg people to throw in all their wasted hours.
> — *Bernard Berenson*

The road to someday leads to a town called nowhere.
> — *Unknown*

Day, *n.* A period of twenty-four hours, mostly misspent.
> — *Ambrose Pierce*

It's not enough to be busy, so are the ants. The question is, what are we busy about?
> — *Henry David Thoreau*

The bad news is time flies. The good news is you're the pilot.
> — *Michael Altshuler*

Amateurs sit and wait for inspiration, the rest of us just get up and go to work.
> — *Stephen King*

Be like a postage stamp. Stick to it until you get there.
> — *Harvey Mackay*

We cannot do everything at once, but we can do something at once.
> —*Calvin Coolidge*

Chapter 7
Recruit cheerleaders

Don't hang out with negative people — including yourself.
— Beth Mende Conny

To bring a dream to life, we must enter unknown territory. Having supporters to cheer us on makes our travels less frightening.

Ideally, these folks will lend us their ears and hearts; offer suggestions and a shoulder to cry on; build us up, not tear us down. They will journey with us and benefit from our efforts, directly or indirectly. It doesn't always happen that way, of course. We may well have to ask, prod and teach them to give us the support we need. Even the most enthusiastic among them will occasionally lose their patience and say, "Enough of your crazy ideas. Wash the dishes." But so it goes. And so we must go, solo if need be.

But it rarely turns out that way. If we are smart about it and discriminating, we will surround ourselves with the right people.

Choose your audiences
"Choose your audiences carefully," my father once told me. It was one of the best pieces of advice I have ever received. Although he was a writer, he was not talking about readers but people in general.

He believed you should carefully choose the people with whom you share your ideas, most especially when ideas are taking shape. Negative people will say you are unrealistic, perhaps delusional, and they will tick off a list of reasons why you will fail. They will speak with such authority that you may start believing them.

But — and pay attention here — it is not *their* fault. It is yours. You chose the wrong audience. Yeah, yeah, it was an honest mistake. But chances are you have made the mistake before, perhaps with the same people. You were, shall we say, being dumb.

So let's smarten you up. Let us use the *Supporters Inventory* to help you make better choices. Simply list people you know and interact with regularly or less regularly but in a substantive way. Exclude those you speak with only in passing (e.g., cashiers, mechanics, bus drivers, salespeople, doctors, librarians, etc.). Also exclude people you interact with on Facebook, via Twitter and other social media unless you have an ongoing, meaningful relationship. Examples:

- Spouse/partner
- Mother, father
- Children
- Siblings
- Cousins, aunts, uncles, grandparents
- Friends
- Neighbors
- Priests/rabbis/etc.
- Coworkers/employers/employees
- People you have lost touch with but who are still significant in your life

Now rate each person on how good an "audience" he/she is or would be. You will do so on a scale from 1 to 10, with 1 being the lowest score possible and 10 being the highest.

Supporters Inventory

Name	Score	Name	Score

Next, review your *Supporters Inventory*, comparing scores between and among individuals.

Don't be surprised if some of the people you love most receive low scores. Sometimes their very closeness is problematic. They may not fully understand your project or the effect it will have on them, for if you change, they too will be forced to change. They may resent your needing time alone or may want to protect you from rejection. They may be too busy or caught up in their own lives to care as deeply as you do about your project, or to care at all. None of these things makes them bad people or bad-for-you people. It just makes them people you reach out to less often (if at all).

Here are interesting questions to ask yourself as you review your scores:

• What patterns, if any, do you notice among your scores? For example: your scores are low overall: four of your five best friends get low scores; all of your siblings get high scores.

• Which three individuals received the highest and lowest scores? What in your relationships accounts for the differences?

• Are the scores of some individuals variable? For instance, a parent may score a 3 when it comes to you moving to Ireland but a 9 if you decide to earn your Ph.D.

One last question and perhaps the most difficult: If you were to rate yourself, what would your score be? In other words, are you your best or worst audience?

"Pestimists"

"Pestimists" are those pesty, pessimistic people who make you question your actions, abilities and dreams. They play in the background like Muzak — barely noticeable yet incredibly potent. Undoubtedly, there are some of them on your Supporters List.

The messages Pestimists deliver vary from person to person; however, the words often go like this:

- "You can't do X, Y, Z."
- "No one cares what you have to say."
- "You don't have the talent, money or persistence to complete your project."
- "You're wasting your time on a pipe dream."

Now that you know what Pestimists are, here are some suggestions for handling them:

Change your phrasing

Identify your most persistent Pestimist and articulate his or her message. For example: "No one will want to read your novel."

Next, turn that statement into a question. For instance: "What makes you think anyone will want to read your novel?" Now answer the question: "I don't know if someone will or won't read my novel, but right now, all I am going to do is concentrate on finishing it."

Why this progression? Because Pestimists want you to question yourself. Here, at last, you have an opportunity to answer them.

Give your Pestimist a face

Because it's easier to deal with an adversary you can see, give your Pestimist a face. Find a photo of the close family member, friend or co-worker who undermines your confidence (whether they realize it or not). Or skim newspapers, magazines and circulars for a face that matches your Pestimist's personality. Tape the photo onto an index card and keep it in a handy place. When your Pestimist comes calling, turn over the index card. This is a subtle but conscious act. It puts your Pestimist on notice that you are no longer listening.

Become a stern parent

Treat your Pestimist like the kid who threatens to throw a tantrum if she doesn't get your immediate attention. Say to her: "I will listen to you as soon as I finish what I am doing — and only when I am finished. I'll be done in X amount of time. You'll either have to sit quietly or get lost until then." (By the way, when dealing with Pestimists, any amount of time you can negotiate for yourself — be it only minutes — is a tremendous feat.)

Be understanding

Accept your Pestimist's good intentions. Often, Pestimists are not trying to be negative as much as protective, much like parents. For example, think back to the days when you first got your license and wanted to borrow the family car. Chances are you went through a grilling: "Where are you off to? With whom? What time will you be back?" The greater your ability to calm your parents' fears, the more likely you would be to get the car keys. The same holds true for Pestimists. To undertake a project is to go off in a whole new direction, and it's their job to keep you safe. And so you have to let them know what you're up to and how you will proceed. Be realistic about your goals and you'll give your Pestimists less to worry about. It's like telling your parents you'll be driving to the movies rather than driving cross country.

Partnering up

Should we have too many low scorers on our "Supporters Inventory," it may be time to find new cheerleaders. That may require that we move beyond our circle to find like-minded people via the Web and social media, or by networking or joining workshops and clubs. Sometimes it is just a matter of becoming more aware of the people around us. Who have we overlooked or dismissed too quickly? Is there someone we would like to know but are too shy to approach? Is there someone who may be willing to partner with us?

For example, a number of years ago, I was leaving my daughter's day care center when another mom approached me. "I hear you're a writer," she said. "Do you want to partner?"

It turned out, she was a landscape painter new in town and fairly new to selling her work, and she wanted to find another creative-type to spur her on. To partner would be to form a working relationship, she said. That meant committing to meeting regularly to set goals, report in and hold each other accountable. Perfect timing, I thought. I was a part-time reporter who wanted to transition to books. I was taking baby steps and needed to pick up the pace.

Here's the format we came up with and it worked brilliantly:

- We met for two hours every other week, alternating homes. We each got an hour of that time, alternating who went first.

- Our respective one-hour slots were divided into two 30-minute slots. During the first 30-minute slot, we, respectively, reported on what we had (or hadn't) accomplished. We allowed ourselves to complain and make excuses, discuss fears and blocks, and share personal issues, especially as they affected our creative output (e.g., the 10 days spent caring for a child with chicken pox).

- During our second 30-minute slot, we opened the floor to discussion. We helped each other set or reframe goals, brainstorm and strategize, consider the pros and cons of particular projects and contracts, etc. As importantly, we ended our slots with a commitment: "I will do X, Y and / or Z by the next time we meet."

Over two years of meetings, we both made great strides. She was selling her art in galleries and was also doing commissioned paintings. I published my first book and was at work on my second.

Could we have accomplished these things on our own? I'd like to think so. But the fact is that we did it together. Our partnership worked because we cheered each other on.

By the way: A year or so after we met, I moved out of state and we lost touch. She's still painting, however, and I'm still writing. Our partnership lives on.

Asking for help

At some point during your project, you will need to ask for help. Obviously, you will want to choose the right individuals for advice. But you should also be smart about when and how you do it.

Choose the right time.

Prematurely going public with a project makes you vulnerable because you do not yet "own" the project. You are giving others too much power. A thumbs-down early in the game may stall or even devastate you. Therefore, do not approach anyone until you are truly ready for feedback. There are exceptions to this, of course. For example, if you are working on a skills-based project like building a boat, you do not want to wait until after the boat is nearly finished.

You should also choose your time wisely. Just as we have times of day when we are at our best, so, too, do others. *That* is the time to approach them. Also be aware of people's moods and stress level. No one wants to think, let alone listen, when they are tired or preoccupied.

Choose your team carefully.

One person's opinion is, well, one person's opinion; it may or may not have validity. Two or more people saying the same thing, even in different ways, is harder to dismiss.

Ideally, you will pick individuals with relevant experiences, areas of expertise and/or tastes. Each will come at his or her task from a unique perspective, adding an invaluable dimension to your project. These varying perspectives can also help pinpoint holes in logic and substance, as well as raise overlooked issues.

Let people know what you want and why.

What is it you want? Information? A critique? Ideas? Clarify this before approaching others, so you get the tailored help you need. If not, you give people carte blanche, and who knows what they will throw in. For example, if one of your chosen team is a family member, he or she may find a way to make your project's shortcomings into one of *your* shortcomings or to bring up unrelated issues.

Never ask black or white questions.

By this I mean yes/no or thumbs-up/thumbs-down questions. It is like asking someone if they are for or against you. People generally fall somewhere in-between. Instead, ask open-ended questions: "How can I improve on this idea?" Or, better still, "Can you suggest three ways to improve on this idea?" This will also help others frame their thinking and, thereby, their responses.

Understand the difference between constructive and destructive criticism.

Constructive criticism makes you ponder and, ultimately, improve your project. Destructive criticism saps you of energy and confidence and sets up hurdles and blocks that slow or halt your progress. Plus, they hurt. Constructive criticism is to be embraced; destructive criticism is to be ignored.

Criticism, however constructive, can be hard to take. Nonetheless, it is imperative that you take it well, even with grace and style. If you have chosen the right team, it ain't personal.

Take two steps back.

Feedback takes time to sort through — and that is just fine. In fact, it's preferable. Let the comments of others filter through your system. Let them intermingle. Only when you've fully absorbed the information you have received can you decide how (or even if) you will act on it. Besides, you don't have to do anything right away or at all. You are allowed to disagree, but don't jump the gun. With time, you may come to accept the feedback's legitimacy.

Consult your most important advisor.

Team members will respond to you from their own world view. But your view is just as valid. After all, you know your project better than anyone else. You are the one, *the only one*, who can deliver on its promise. Sure the comments of others count, and, yeah, they can be helpful. Ultimately, however, you are the one in charge. You have the final say.

Recruit cheerleaders!

You are who you surround yourself with.
> — *Selena Gomez*

If you put a small value on yourself, rest assured that the world will
not raise your price.
> — *Anonymous*

I will not let anyone walk through my mind with their dirty feet.
> — *Mahatma Gandhi*

You may be the only person left who believes in you, but it's enough.
It takes just one star to pierce a universe of darkness.
> — *Richelle E. Goodrich*

I'm not a wannabe. I'm a who I wannabe.
> — *Hawk Nelson*

A low self-image is usually not based upon facts; it's mismanaged
memory.
> — *Orrin Woodward*

Believe in yourself and the world will follow suit.
> — *Tadahiko Nagao*

Don't be afraid of opposition. Remember, a kite rises against, not
with, the wind.
> — *Hamilton Mabie*

Chapter 8
Unblock creative blocks

If you are going to doubt something, doubt your limits.
— *Don Ward*

I may not know about a lot of things in life, but I consider myself an expert on creative blocks. I have had to grapple with them my entire writing life — which, aggravatingly, is a good thing. To sail through projects is a sign that I am getting trapped in my comfort zone. I want to grow, forge new ground, leap tall buildings in a single bound! Which means I have to deal with my fears.

And so in this chapter I share my insights and suggestions. My goal is to help you better understand your blocks and take them less personally. Blocks, you see, have nothing to do with talent — please remember this. Rather, they are fears solidified. But that doesn't mean you have to bash through them. Ouch! Sometimes chipping away will do.

From Step A to bbbbbb

One day my college roommate, Robin, and I were hiking in the woods and came upon a stream. A log had fallen over it, providing us a natural bridge. It was a thick tree, easy to walk across and only a couple of feet above the stream.

Robin was, and I assume still is, a natural athlete, one of those people who could bike, ski and dive before she could walk. She practically skipped across the log. I meanwhile inched across it. (I'm a city girl; crossing streets is my idea of sport.) I felt as if I were on a tightrope made of floss.

Robin watched and waited and finally said, "Don't worry about falling. No matter where you step, you're always somewhere."

She was right. It isn't as if I were going to fall into *nothing*. Worse case, I would fall into the water, get wet and wade to the other side. I crossed the log.

Minor as that experience may seem, it taught me a lesson about the fear of missteps, how they can make you freeze, be it on a log or in life. It is a lesson that also applies to dream projects.

A fear of missteps can morph into creative blocks. But *there are no missteps when you create*; there are only steps. As my roommate wisely noted, we are always *somewhere*, and from there we self-correct.

Let's say you want to get from Step A to Step B to Step C. Simple:

$$A - B - C$$

But sometimes the progression is more complicated. You actually have several options:

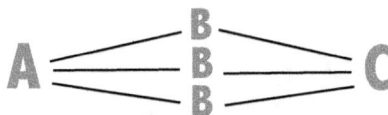

What now? Unfortunately, there may be no easy answer. It may be that all of them are correct. Or several of them. Or one of them. Or none of them. There is only one way to find out. You use your best judgment and make a move. If it proves to be the wrong one, you self-correct.

Self-correction may take time, which can be frustrating and scary. It is at this point that many individuals lose patience and heart and drop their projects. This is a shame, for had they allowed themselves to explore their options, they would have made it from Step B to Step C. *Please don't be one of those people.*

Bounce-back time

Rejection sucks. It should be outlawed. Anyone who challenges your abilities should be tarred and feathered and made to feel as badly as you do. And then they should be forced to apologize on YouTube: "I was an idiot. This person is brilliant. We should name a country after him or her!"

The likelihood of that is slim, of course. (Perhaps a village?) What is definite is that you will feel crummy. There is no way around it, so don't put your energy into trying to make yourself immune. Energy is finite. Use it for other things, namely, for working to decrease your bounce-back time.

Bounce-back time is the amount of time it takes for you to get back on your feet after a rejection. An example:

When I was first starting my writing career, I sent my very first short story to *Mademoiselle,* a national women's magazine. The manuscript was promptly returned with a form rejection. I buried both it and my story in my filing cabinet.

About six months later, I toyed with the idea of circulating the story again and reread the rejection letter. Huh? There, scrawled at the bottom, a personal note from the editor. She apologized for not taking my piece, which, in fact, she liked — a lot. It didn't make the cut, however, because the magazine took only one story a month, 12 stories a year. Nonetheless, she encouraged me to submit other work. How had I not seen this? Easy: Rejection blinded me.

Were this to happen today, I'd still feel terrible — but it wouldn't take me six months to bounce back. I have since shortened my bounce-back time.

Exercise

Think about your dream project. How long of a bounce-back time would you need? A few days or weeks? A month or two? Guesstimate. Be optimistic. What's the worst that could happen? That you exceed the amount of time you had set? But at least you have set a time limit. This gives you something to measure yourself against. After all, you don't want to wait a month, when you believe it possible to get back on your feet within a couple of weeks.

Set goals within goals

What if someone were to tell you that you could not fail. It was impossible. Guaranteed. He or she would even be willing to bet you a million bucks. Tempting offer, eh? But what's the catch? There is one, but it's easy and legal. You may actually enjoy it. It can be summed up in four words — set goals within goals.

Here's what you do:

1) Write down your ultimate goal (e.g., move to Ireland, climb Mt. Everest, open a bakery, write a novel).

For demonstration purposes, I'll use "Move to Ireland." That's a great goal but a huge one, so huge, in fact, that it's unachievable without first breaking it into steps. One step is to make an extended visit to Ireland to determine where you would want to live. You will also need to create an itinerary, if only to know which city you will fly into. To create an itinerary, you likely will need to ask for recommendations, read travel guides, watch videos and do online searches. You'll also need to arrange time off of work and to get a passport.

As you can see — and as I am sure you have experienced with less ambitious goals — the number of steps can multiply quickly. And that's a good thing, for the greater your ability to break a goal into steps, the greater the likelihood of success.

Here's what we've got so far:

> **Ultimate goal:** Relocate to Ireland
>
> **Step:** Make extended visit to Ireland
>
> **Step:** Research places to visit
>
> **Step:** Create itinerary
>
> **Step:** Arrange time off work
>
> **Step:** Get passport
>
> **Step:** Make airline reservation

2) Now, let's change our wording. Instead of "step," let's use the term "goal within goal."

The change is subtle but meaningful. Steps *are* goals — goals *within* an ultimate goal. Each is achieveable, not at some distant time — like the goal to move to Ireland — but now, or close to now. Achieving goals within goals makes failure impossible. Rather, it builds confidence and momentum.

Here then is our list of goals within goals:

    Ultimate goal: Relocate to Ireland

        Goal within goal: Make extended visit to Ireland

        Goal within goal: Research places to visit

        Goal within goal: Create itinerary

        Goal within goal: Arrange time off work

        Goal within goal: Get passport

        Goal within goal: Make airline reservation

Note: Even these goals have goals within them. Keep breaking them down until each is a manageable size. You know you've reached the right size when the goal doesn't overwhelm you.

3) Now it's your turn to create goals within goals, using the worksheet on the next page. Check off each goal as you complete it. There are additional blank sheets in the Appendix.

Tried and true approaches to unblocking

As one who has the dubious distinction of blocking frequently, I have had to develop strategies for regaining my momentum. Here are some I find particularly helpful.

Expect failure

This sounds negative but it's not. At some point you *will* get sidetracked or derailed; you *will* experience failure. But remember: an experience is simply an experience; it is not failure itself. That said, instead of waiting for the worst to happen, whatever that may be, devise strategies for dealing with possible snags. Identify what they may be and ways to get around them. Create a list of individuals you will turn to for advice and support. Make a list of fun activities that will divert your attention as you give your mind a rest. (I find chocolate a great fallback.)

Goals Within Goals

Ultimate goal _____

_____

   ❏ Goal within goal: _____

   _____

   ❏ Goal within goal: _____

   _____

   ❏ Goal within goal: _____

   _____

   ❏ Goal within goal: _____

   _____

   ❏ Goal within goal:

   _____

Lower the stakes

Wonderful as your project may be, it's not going to change the world. Hang onto that idea, however, and you raise the stakes impossibly high. You cannot complete an impossible project.

Shift the spotlight

Don't make your project about *you*. Make it about someone else or something else. Think of it as a beautifully wrapped present or a heartfelt thank-you to the world; a way to make the world a better, sweeter place.

Go on a diet

Forget cutting back on carbs. Go on a negativity-free diet. For one week, even one day, don't read the newspapers, turn on the TV or get on the Internet. Avoid people who bring you down or dull your senses. Keep negativity out and your project will come back in.

Work softer, not harder

Working hard is hard work. It may make you think you're getting someplace — no pain, no gain — but really you are just staying put. You can't ram your way through a block; you'll knock yourself out. Work softer instead. That may mean doing the easy stuff first or doing less than you had planned. Both, however, can make you a lot more productive.

Go on sabbatical

Sometimes, you simply need a break, so go on sabbatical. But determine for how long. A few days? A week? A month? (More time than that and you're pushing it.) Like a professor, you should use the time constructively. Take a vacation or a class, play guitar or soccer with your kids. Catch up on sleep, run a marathon. Do nothing (which may be your biggest challenge of all).

Go through the motions

You don't need divine inspiration to work on your project. Nor do you need passion. You just need to keep at it. Write that paragraph, hammer that nail, read that textbook, practice that song, work that field — trudge on. As with other things in life, you do what you have to do. Down the line there is a benefit, even if you are just going through the motions.

Unanswered prayers

One of my favorite country songs is Garth Brooks's "Unanswered Prayers." It is about a guy who bumps into his high school sweetheart while he and his wife attend a hometown football game. He thinks back on the woman, his first true love, and how he'd pray to God to make her love him. But as he and his old girlfriend talk, he realizes time has changed both of them; she's not the woman he would want to spend his life with. He turns and looks at his wife and realizes she, in fact, is the greatest gift in his life. And he thanks God for unanswered prayers.

Corny as this song may be, it got me thinking about unanswered prayers. Roads not taken. Relationships ended. Places left behind. Words said, unsaid. It also got me thinking about my various projects over the years — how at times things seemed to be going wrong, when actually they were going right. It just took time to realize it.

And so it may be that your creative block is really an unanswered prayer. When well-laid plans come undone and all seems lost, you may well discover that you are, indeed, on the right path.

Unblock creative blocks!

It is hard to fight an enemy who has outposts in your head.
— *Sally Kempton*

Creativity is allowing yourself to make mistakes. Art is knowing which ones to keep.
— *Scott Adams*

Not all those who wander are lost.
— *J.R.R. Tolkien*

Anxiety is the handmaiden of creativity.
— *T.S. Eliot*

An objection is not a rejection; it is simply a request for more information.
— *Bo Bennett*

It's not who you are that holds you back, it's who you think you're not.
—*Unknown*

Nothing reduces the odds against you like ignoring them.
— *Richard Brault*

chapter 9
Claim your space

In solitude the mind gains strength and learns to lean upon itself.
— *Laurence Sterne*

Our projects need not just time but space. A space we can call our own. But where do we find it? How much do we need? Is space even physical? Let's explore.

Designated space

Although it would be great to have a designated space, do you really need it? If you are training to hike the Appalachian Trail, for example, you don't need an office. If you are renovating a house, the house itself may be your office. What you might need, instead, is designated space: a place to store your gear and guidebooks, or lay out your architectural drawings and paint chips.

Designated space is easier to come by than, say, a separate room. It can be a corner of a room or even just a table — but it is yours. No one else messes with it.

You can find such space by re-familiarizing yourself with your home or workplace. Observe usage closely. What space is being unused or under-utilized. Perhaps it is a bedroom corner or a basement closet. How can you convert it to suit your needs?

Pay particular attention to redundant spaces like dining rooms and kitchens, and family rooms and living rooms. Do you use both equally? Can you get by with just one? If not, why? Ditto furniture. Do you really need more than one couch? Are matching end tables necessary? What items can you move elsewhere, toss or give to a friend as a "permanent loan"?

Re-purposed space

Can you change the "purpose" of certain spaces? A great example of this is the master bedroom. Yeah, it's got great amenities like a separate bathroom, but, ultimately, it is simply a place to sleep. Even if you have a king-sized bed (which measures 76" x 80"), you have oceans of space remaining, which too often is filled with dressers, chairs and end tables you do not really need.

Try using that space for other purposes. For example, when an artist friend of mine set up a home studio, she chose the basement because it was the only space available. It had little light, however, and was inconvenient because she needed easy access to a sink. Ultimately, she moved her studio into the master bedroom, and she and her husband slept in the guest room. (They had visitors only a few times a year.)

Timed space

If you can only work on your project weekday mornings from 7-9 a.m., or on Saturday afternoons, then you might not need a 24/7 space (not that it wouldn't be great). If you are working on a limited-time project (e.g., building bird houses for an annual crafts fair), you might not need anything 365 days of the year.

Should you not have a set schedule, you may be able to access (grab!) space when it becomes available. My mother, a single mom and writer, did just that. When she began work on her novel, she worked whenever she had the apartment to herself. That often meant getting up and writing from 5-7 a.m. on school days, when my sister and I were still asleep, and on Sundays, when my father took us for the day. It took her five years to finish her novel. Her efforts paid off, however. She sold her book to a major publisher. (If that's not proof of how you can make a dream come true, even if you have only slivers of time and space, I don't know what is!)

Multiple spaces

My first office was a wooden door, crammed into the corner of my living room and perched on wobbly sawhorses. My second office was an unheated laundry room attached to the three-room house my husband and I rented. The concrete floor was buckled and water seeped under the door when it rained, forcing me to shut off my computer and space heater. My third office was a desk in my infant's bedroom. Surrounded by toys, diaper boxes and unfolded laundry, I worked around her sleep schedule.

Today, I have a great office. No leaks, no toys. I've earned it. But I don't always work in it. That's because I consider it my left-brained space. It's where I go when I'm ready to shape my right-brain musings into books, articles, Web posts, etc.

My right-brained office is actually several offices: my shower, bed, dining room table, living room couch and favorite table at a local café. I also have an outdoor office, which is my neighborhood. I do some of my best thinking while walking.

All of which is to say that instead of one space, you may be able to find several. So start keeping track of your wanderings. Note where ideas are most apt to come to you: the gym, kitchen, subway, lunchroom, corner bar, den, bathroom ... Once you identify them, think about how you can use these "hot spots" to your advantage.

Portable space

Space is something you can fit into a box. Literally. For example, instead of filing cabinets, I often use large cardboard boxes for my writing projects. Filing is too much work and takes too much time, and so I tuck papers into boxes, one project to a box, along with other materials: notebooks, reference books, and a plastic bag filled with pens, markers, stickies, paperclips and a miniature stapler.

Another great thing is that my box is portable. It enables me to take my project wherever I go — dining room, the café, my in-laws' home, on vacation, etc. Everything I need is at my disposal. And when I am done for the day, I close the lid and store the box in the closet, or under my bed or desk. When I am working on several projects, I stack the boxes in the corner of my office.

This approach only works for portable projects, of course, but you may be able to divide your project into smaller pieces to carry around. Other items you can fit in a box include: manuals, digital recorders and cameras, art supplies, toolkits, laptops, tablets, small printers and scanners, and chocolates (one of my necessities).

The most important space of all — mental space

A project needs mental space, a place to call home. You must treat it as a guest and not make it sleep on the floor. Let it take up residence in your mind; let it spread out its belongings.

Mental space also is sacred space and must be protected. But be forewarned: Doing so can make you unpopular. People will get impatient and angry, or they may feel rejected. Be ready to compromise, to let them visit when *you* see fit, and only if you know they won't tear up the place with resentment or negativity.

Be prepared to live alone at times, times when your creative juices flow and your energy level swells; times when you need distance, so you can hear yourself speak, hear your project speak to you, saying, "I am ready. Help me *be.*"

Claim your space!

Being solitary is being alone well.
— *Alice Koller*

People who violate your boundaries are thieves. They steal time that doesn't belong to them.
— *Elizabeth Grace Saunders*

Honouring your own boundaries is the clearest message to others to honor them, too.
— *Gina Greenlee*

Here in your mind you have complete privacy. Here there's no difference between what is and what could be.
— *Chuck Palahniuk*

Your personal boundaries protect the inner core of your identity and your right to choices.
— *Gerard Manley Hopkins*

When trying to teach someone a boundary, they learn less from the enforcement of the boundary and more from the way the boundary was established.
— *Bryant H. McGill*

Chapter 10
Embrace happy surprises

Life is surprise, nothing else.
— *Unknown*

A number of years ago, I took a painting class for fun. Our first in-class assignment was to paint a still life: a cup, pitcher and bowl of fruit on a tablecloth. I started with the pitcher but couldn't get it right; my colors were off. But as soon as I fixed them, my shading was off. I fixed my shading but then the position of the pitcher was off, which threw off the colors ... One hour later, and I was still at it.

When my instructor came over, I shared my frustration. He nodded and suggested I try a different approach. "Forget the pitcher," he said. "Take in the *whole* still life. Sketch it out in broad brush strokes so you see how everything relates. If you only focus on the pitcher, you'll miss out on happy surprises."

Happy surprises. I love that expression! How well it relates to creative projects. The importance of giving up control so you can open yourself to ah-ha moments; those spot-on insights that make the heart sing and planets align. I wish you dozens of these. Keep at it and you will have them. Guaranteed.

Next steps

I'd like to think I am leaving you in good hands — your own. But should you need a bit of direction for how to proceed, let me make a few suggestions.

- Make *Fearless Creativity* your project bible. Choose a "passage" and apply it to your creative life. That passage could be a chapter, section, exercise or simply a quotation. The key is to *do* something with it. *Any* step you take is a step forward.

- Review all chapters periodically. It is akin to getting an annual physical; you want to make sure your project is healthy. Do not wait for a year to pass, however. Check in every few weeks. Schedule it on your calendar. It is a great way to take your project's pulse.

- I *strongly* recommend that you review these two chapters weekly:
  — Chapter 5, "Strategize success." As I discussed, it is critical that you break a project into the smallest steps possible. This will make your goals manageable and boost your courage. Identify the steps and, voila!, you've figured out your strategy.
  — Chapter 6, "Protect your time." Time is a resource waiting to be mined. The techniques in this chapter will remind you where to find it.

- When you feel yourself stall or block — and it *will* happen — return to Chapter 8, "Unblock creative blocks." But you will also want to review Chapter 3, "Challenge your fears." Remember, blocks are fears solidified. Identify and work through your fears and you will unblock.

- Get support. Buddies, fellow travelers, rabid cheerleaders. Follow the suggestions I outline in Chapter 7, "Recruit cheerleaders." Keep on the lookout for like-minded souls you can partner with.

- Form a *Fearless Creativity* support group. Meet regularly to share your dreams and "report in" on your progress. Read and discuss sections of the book and develop ways to put what you've learned to good use.

- Each day, choose one of the inspirational quotes sprinkled throughout the book. Personalize the quote. Put it into action.

Keep in touch!

Include me among your cheerleaders. Drop me an e-mail and let me know how you and your projects are doing. I'd especially like to hear about:

- Creative ways you get your juices flowing
- Fears that stymie you, as well as fears you have overcome
- Your strategies for finding the time and space you need
- Effective techniques for working through creative blocks
- Inspirational quotations others would enjoy

You can contact me at *Beth@WriteDirections.com*. And don't forget to visit *WriteDirections.com*, which has great resources for writers and other creative souls.

I look forward to developing our relationship. In the meantime, and as captain of your cheerleading squad, here's my sincerest of cheers — Go! Go! Go!

Embrace happy surprises!

Surprise is key in all art.
— *Oscar Niemeyer*

Expect nothing. Live frugally on surprise.
— *Alice Walker*

The moments of happiness we enjoy take us by surprise. It is not that we seize them, but that they seize us.
— *Ashley Montagu*

The only thing that should surprise us is that there are still some things that can surprise us.
— *Francois de La Rochefoucauld*

Life is full of surprises; however, they are nothing to a mind that shelters positive beliefs.
— *Edmond Mbiaka*

Wherever you go, no matter what the weather, always bring your own sunshine.
— *Anthony J. D'Angelo*

Appendix
Worksheets

De-habit List

1. _____

2. _____

3. _____

4. _____

5. _____

De-habit List

1. _____

2. _____

3. _____

4. _____

5. _____

I am afraid that/of ...

_____

_____

_____

_____

_____

_____

_____

_____

_____

_____

I am afraid that/of ...

Acts of Courage

Acts of Courage

_____

_____

_____

_____

_____

_____

_____

_____

_____

_____

Dream Projects

Dream Projects

Your **Dream Project Criteria Worksheet**

Projects	Expertise	Money	Time	Support	Passion	TOTALS
TOTALS						

Your Dream Project Criteria Worksheet

Projects	Expertise	Money	Time	Support	Passion	TOTALS
TOTALS						

Your **Project Steps**

Steps

	Beginning	Middle	End

Your **Project Steps**

Steps

	Beginning	Middle	End

Daily Activities Log

12 a.m.	12 p.m.
1 a.m.	1 p.m.
2 a.m.	2 p.m.
3 a.m.	3 p.m.
4 a.m.	4 p.m.
5 a.m.	5 p.m.
6 a.m.	6 p.m.
7 a.m.	7 p.m.
8 a.m.	8 p.m.
9 a.m.	9 p.m.
10 a.m.	10 p.m.
11 a.m.	11 p.m.

Daily Activities Log

12 a.m.	12 p.m.
1 a.m.	1 p.m.
2 a.m.	2 p.m.
3 a.m.	3 p.m.
4 a.m.	4 p.m.
5 a.m.	5 p.m.
6 a.m.	6 p.m.
7 a.m.	7 p.m.
8 a.m.	8 p.m.
9 a.m.	9 p.m.
10 a.m.	10 p.m.
11 a.m.	11 p.m.

Weekly Activities Log

Sunday	
Monday	
Tuesday	
Wednesday	
Thursday	
Friday	
Saturday	

Weekly Activities Log

Sunday
Monday
Tuesday
Wednesday
Thursday
Friday
Saturday

Supporters Inventory

Name	Score	Name	Score

Supporters Inventory

Name	Score	Name	Score

Goals Within Goals

Ultimate goal _____

_____

❑ **Goal within goal:** _____

_____

❑ **Goal within goal:** _____

_____

❑ **Goal within goal:** _____

_____

❑ **Goal within goal:** _____

_____

❑ **Goal within goal:**

_____

Goals Within Goals

Ultimate goal _____

_____

❏ **Goal within goal:** _____

_____

❏ **Goal within goal:** _____

_____

❏ **Goal within goal:** _____

_____

❏ **Goal within goal:** _____

_____

❏ **Goal within goal:**

_____

Acknowledgements

Never-ending thanks to my fearless family
Joe, Julia and Jenna

My fearless cheerleaders
Ivonne Anglin, Sharon Cool, Betsy Hall, Judy Korotkin,
Anne Ludwig, Nina Mende, Sheree Parris Nudd, Connie Pryor,
Karen Smith Racicot, Michele Wong, Whitney Yount

My fearless clients
whose courage to live their dreams
inspires and strengthens me

About the author
Beth Mende Conny

Being creative is our nature and right — our way of saying to the world, I am here. I matter.

That's the philosophy I live by and the one that has shaped my writing, speaking and consulting.

I came up through the writing ranks as a newspaper reporter, feature writer and syndicated columnist. Along the way, I fell in love with books and have since written, edited, ghosted and helped others produce more than four dozen of them, more than a million copies of which are in print.

I am also the founder of WriteDirections.com, where writers and creative souls like you can get the tips, tools and inspiration you need to bring dream projects to life. At the site you can sign up for my monthly newsletter and learn more about my books, consulting and public speaking services. You'll also find WriteDirections on Facebook.

Let's stay in touch! Email me your success stories, or even your setbacks. I'd love to share your experiences with others, so they too can become fearless and proudly state: *I am here. I matter.*

Beth Mende Conny
WriteDirections.com
Beth@WriteDirections.com

www.ingramcontent.com/pod-product-compliance
Lightning Source LLC
LaVergne TN
LVHW021521080426
835509LV00018B/2586